WAL

HOWARDIAN
HILLS

HILLSIDE GUIDES - ACROSS NORTHERN ENGLAND

The Uplands of Britain - full colour hardback books
- THE HIGH PEAKS OF ENGLAND & WALES
- YORKSHIRE DALES, MOORS & FELLS

Hillwalking - Lake District
- LAKELAND FELLS - SOUTH
- LAKELAND FELLS - EAST
- LAKELAND FELLS - NORTH
- LAKELAND FELLS - WEST

Long Distance Walks
- COAST TO COAST WALK
- DALES WAY
- CUMBRIA WAY
- WESTMORLAND WAY
- FURNESS WAY
- LADY ANNE'S WAY
- BRONTE WAY
- CALDERDALE WAY
- PENDLE WAY
- CLEVELAND WAY
- NIDDERDALE WAY
- TRANS-PENNINE WAY

Circular Walks - Yorkshire Dales
- WHARFEDALE
- MALHAMDALE
- SWALEDALE
- NIDDERDALE
- THREE PEAKS
- WENSLEYDALE
- HOWGILL FELLS
- HARROGATE & WHARFE VALLEY
- RIPON & LOWER WENSLEYDALE

Circular Walks - Peak District
- NORTHERN PEAK
- CENTRAL PEAK
- EASTERN PEAK
- SOUTHERN PEAK
- WESTERN PEAK

Circular Walks - Lancashire/North West
- BOWLAND
- PENDLE & THE RIBBLE
- WEST PENNINE MOORS
- ARNSIDE & SILVERDALE

Circular Walks - North Pennines
- TEESDALE
- EDEN VALLEY
- ALSTON & ALLENDALE

Circular Walks - North York Moors/York area
- WESTERN MOORS
- SOUTHERN MOORS
- HOWARDIAN HILLS

Circular Walks - South Pennines
- ILKLEY MOOR
- BRONTE COUNTRY
- CALDERDALE
- SOUTHERN PENNINES

---

*Send for a detailed current catalogue and price list
and also visit www.hillsidepublications.co.uk*

WALKING COUNTRY

—————

HOWARDIAN HILLS

Paul Hannon

—————

Hillside

HILLSIDE
PUBLICATIONS
20 Wheathead Crescent
Keighley
West Yorkshire
BD22 6LX

First published 2008

© Paul Hannon 2008

ISBN 978-1-870141-85-7

Cover illustration: River Derwent and Kirkham Abbey
Back cover:
Hovingham; Crayke; Kilburn White Horse from Husthwaite
Page One: The Mausoleum, Castle Howard
Page Three: Cottage at Bulmer
(Paul Hannon/Hillslides Picture Library)

The sketch maps in this book are based upon
1947 Ordnance Survey One-Inch maps

Printed in Great Britain by
Carnmor Print
95-97 London Road
Preston
Lancashire
PR1 4BA

CONTENTS

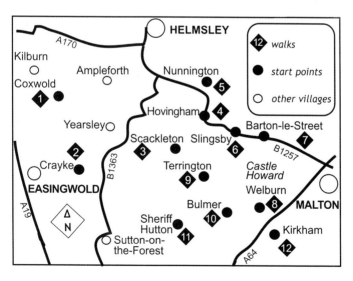

INTRODUCTION

The Howardian Hills Area of Outstanding Natural Beauty sits to the north of the great city of York between the country towns of Malton, Helmsley and Easingwold. Designated in 1987 it comprises a mere 79 square miles, taking its name from the famous stately home that nestles amid this rolling countryside, Castle Howard. This seemingly secretive setting adjoining the southern limit of the North York Moors National Park is a peaceful world of sleepy villages and woodland breaking up an agricultural landscape. The rivers Rye and Derwent flow at the northern and southernmost extremities, while the tiny Foss wriggles through bound for York. At the heart are lovely villages such as Crayke, Terrington and Hovingham; magnificent houses at Nunnington Hall and Newburgh Priory; castle ruins at Slingsby and Sheriff Hutton; glorious old churches such as Stonegrave, Dalby and Appleton-le-Street; and monastic splendour at Kirkham Abbey. Let's get one thing straight - the term 'Hills' is ambitious: the highest point of the area is the village crossroads at Yearsley, a very modest 571ft/174m. While many of the fields have been put to the plough, they are often lined by colourful poppies in summer, and the wide skies ensure a great sense of space and freedom. The area's inviting path network has largely been well preserved, and waymarking is also of a generally high standard.

Access to the countryside

With the exception of a couple of short permissive sections all the walks in this guide are on public rights of way. Availability of any public transport is mentioned in the introduction to each walk. The nearest railway stations are at Malton, York and Thirsk.

Using the guide

Each walk is self contained, with essential information being followed by a concise route description and simple map. Dovetailed in between are notes and illustrations of features along the way. Snippets of information have been placed in *italics* to ensure that the essential route description is easier to locate. The sketch maps serve to identify the location of the routes rather than the fine detail, and whilst the description should be sufficient to guide you around, an Ordnance Survey map is strongly recommended. To gain the most from a walk, the detail of the 1:25,000 scale Explorer maps is unsurpassed. They also gives the option to vary walks as desired, giving an improved picture of your surroundings and the availability of linking paths. One map covers all but two walks:

- *Explorer 300 - Howardian Hills & Malton*
- *Explorer 299 - Ripon & Boroughbridge (Walks 1 and 2 only)*

Also useful for planning is Landranger map 100 (1:50,000 scale).

USEFUL ADDRESSES

Ramblers' Association
2nd Floor, Camelford House, 87-89 Albert Embankment, London SE1 7BR
•020-7339 8500

Howardian Hills AONB office
The Mews, Wath Court, Hovingham, York YO62 4NN
•0845-034 9495

Tourist Information
58 Market Place **Malton** YO17 7LW •01653-600048
De Grey Rooms, Exhibition Square **York** YO1 7HB •01904-621756
Castlegate **Helmsley** YO62 5AB •01439-770173
49 Market Place **Thirsk** YO7 1HA •01845-522755

Public Transport Information
Traveline •0870 608 2608   National Rail Enquiries •08457-484950

Left: The City of Troy maze

1

BEACON BANKS

START *Coxwold   Grid ref. SE 535771*

DISTANCE *5$\frac{1}{4}$ miles (8$\frac{1}{2}$km)*

ORDNANCE SURVEY MAPS
1:50,000
Landranger 100 - Malton & Pickering
1:25,000
Explorer 299 - Ripon & Boroughbridge

ACCESS *Start from the village centre. Car park on the Byland Abbey road. Served by Helmsley-Easingwold-York bus.*

> *Two charming villages are linked by a lovely viewpoint ridge*

Coxwold is a hugely attractive village that was in busier times a market town. Perhaps best known for its literary associations, Shandy Hall was the mid-18th century home of Laurence Sterne, local vicar and the author of 'Tristram Shandy'. The charming red-brick house and gardens are open to the public from May to September. Coxwold's sloping streets are lined by lovely buildings, many of great interest including the Old Hall (a former grammar school of 1603), Colville Hall and some 17th century almshouses. The Fauconberg Arms recalls the original occupants of the nearby mansion of Newburgh Priory: now in the hands of the equally locally influential Wombwell family, it and its grounds are open to view on a limited basis. St Michael's church dates back to the 15th century and occupies a commanding position. There is also a Post office/shop, tearoom and pottery, and a WC at the car park. A split identity makes Coxwold the southernmost village of the North York Moors National Park, though this walk has sections within the AONB, the National Park, and neither!

From the crossroads ascend the main street past the church. *Shandy Hall, incidentally, is just a little further up.* Just past the church cross the end of the green and bear left through a gate along a short-lived driveway. Emerging into a field beyond the houses, bear right. *Ahead is a big sweep of countryside, most notable feature being your return route along colourful Beacon Banks across the valley.* Cross to join a fence, briefly, before a grassy track cuts a corner of the field to run to a gate/stile. By now the Kilburn White Horse and the adjacent scarp of Roulston Scar are displayed over to the right. Advance along the field boundary. *This gentle dome also offers big views ahead to the long line of the Pennines across the flat Vale of York.*

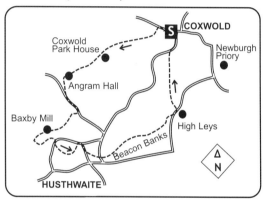

At the end a track drops down the right side of an impassable enclosed way, then resume along the same fieldside with the farm at Coxwold Park House below. Dropping to meets its drive, cross straight over to a gate and down a briefly enclosed way beside trees. Through a small gate at the bottom continue on the fieldside to a stile onto an access road. Advance along this to the farm at Angram Hall, and remain on the main track zigzagging between buildings and out past the house.

After bridging delightfully named Twattleton Beck you have a brief choice. Either opt to remain on the drive up onto the road and go left, or cut a corner by a gate on the left, slanting across the field to a stile onto the road. Either way, go left along the road to quickly reach the course of an old railway. *This was the Thirsk & Malton Branch of the North Eastern Railway from the main line at Pilmoor Junction through the Coxwold-Gilling gap to split, a branch joining the Scarborough line at Malton, and one going north to Helmsley and Pickering. On the right is Husthwaite's old station house.* Immediately across, and just before Elphin Bridge, take a gate on the right and cross a long field parallel with Elphin Beck. From a stile at the far end a little path heads away, swinging round to a stile into the grounds of the house at Baxby Mill. *This presents an intriguing arrangement of outbuildings.*

Advance to the buildings and through a small gate to pass alongside the house to the front, where head away along its grassy drive. This runs out into a field and along to join the track of Ings Lane. Turn left here, bridging the beck and rising to a T-junction. Go left to Baxby Manor and then right on the drive out onto a road on the edge of Husthwaite. While you might go left up the road, better to turn briefly right then left up a track. Quickly leave this on a path forking right to rise pleasantly alongside a tiny stream. On opening out, advance just a little further then cross a small bridge on the stream. Through a little gate an inviting snicket heads away between gardens, later crossing one of them before emerging onto the main street alongside the former schoolhouse.

Just to the left, the Blacksmiths Arms has in recent years become the Roasted Pepper restaurant and bar. Turn right the few yards to the junction. *Husthwaite village centre comprises a delightful triangular green with snowdrops, a central tree and a seat. It is overlooked on one side by the lovely church of St Nicholas, dating from the 12th century, with a 15th century tower and many features of interest. On another side stands a splendid timber-framed cottage.*

Leave by turning right at the green, but as the road starts to climb take a snicket on the left. This enclosed path rises to emerge into a field. Rise to the top corner, and from the kissing-gate bear left up the next fieldside to another such gate, concluding along another snicket out onto a road. Go left a few strides and turn right up a driveway. *With its colourful immediate surrounds and super views across to the White Horse, here begins the finest section of the walk.* Beyond the houses a couple of gates precede the start of a firm path making a gentle rise along the crest of Beacon Banks, running delightfully along to a white Ordnance Survey column. *At 433ft/132m this is marginally overtopped as summit of the walk by a 443ft/135m contour just ahead. To your left the relatively steep slopes are crowded with gorse bushes and newly planted trees that some day will obscure the views. Also below here are some ancient earthworks.*

Resume along the edge with the established trees of Beacon Banks Wood alongside. The path runs on for some time before swinging right to join a back road. Turn down this just as far as the farm at High Leys, then leave by a stile on the left. Drop steeply to a stile in a hedge, then down to the far corner of the field. Through the gate head along the hedgeside to a footbridge in the bottom corner, then continue along the other side. Note the confluence of the two little streams. Part way along take a small stone-arched bridge on the stream to access a gate onto a road. Turn right for the final few minutes back into Coxwold. *At the village edge you cross the old level crossing, noting the wooden crossing box doing sterling service in a garden. Coxwold's station closed in 1964.*

Coxwold

11

RIVER FOSS

START *Crayke   Grid ref. SE 561705*

DISTANCE *5 miles (8km)*

ORDNANCE SURVEY MAPS
1:50,000
Landranger 100 - Malton & Pickering
1:25,000
Explorer 299 - Ripon & Boroughbridge

ACCESS *Start from the village centre. Roadside parking. Served by York-Easingwold bus.*

> *Even by Howardians standards this is a gentle outing, seeking the secretive, youthful Foss from a superb village*

Crayke is a hugely characterful village set on and around the landmark knoll of Castle Hill on which stands its church. Crayke was given by Egfrid, King of Northumberland, to St Cuthbert of Lindisfarne in AD 685 with the aim of founding one of the earliest monasteries in Northern England. The present St Cuthbert's church dates from the 15th century. Either side of it are the red-brick Crayke Hall and the stone-walled Crayke Castle, an imposing house again on the site of a far older building that played host to 13th and 14th century kings. Descending to the Durham Ox pub at the main junction is Church Hill, a steeply sloping green with a riot of daffodils.

From the pub head north along Brandsby Street, descending between rows of charming cottages with red pantile roofs. When they end continue along the road as far as a bend at Mill Green which offers farmhouse preserves, shop and tearoom. Here bear left on a short access road to Crayke Manor. *The big house stands to the left, fronted by a ha-ha.* Advance into a yard with several houses, then turn sharp right on the continuing access road to bridge a stream, your first encounter with the youthful River Foss. *It springs to life above Oulston Reservoir on the western fringe of the Howardian Hills just to the north, and flows a meandering course southwards to merge into the Ouse in the heart of York.*

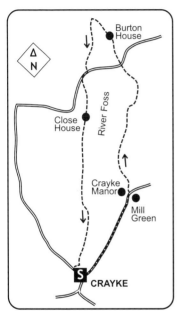

The firm track heads away and runs unfailingly along to Woodfield Farm. En route, at a wood corner the right-of-way briefly breaks off, continuing straight on a fieldside track to a corner stile. Here go right on another short track that rejoins the road to the farm. Over to the left is the tree-lined Foss. Keep straight on past the house, and as the track makes for the vast barns go straight ahead: a little bank crosses the centre of the field to a stile in a hedge ahead. Continue to another stile at a tiny trickle, then advance to the farm at Beckfield House. Passing left to a stile onto its access road, cross straight over and across a field centre to a stile into a clump of trees. Drop down the little clearing into a large field, and a track leads straight across to a gate/stile onto a back road. Cross to a small gate and gently ascend the brow to merge into the access road to Burton House. *Ahead are colourful hill slopes, while big views look out across the flat vale to the distant Pennines.*

Bear left of the house to the last barn, where a gate points you left to a small gate at the bottom corner. Finally closing in on the Foss, bear right to gain it amid woodland featuring ancient hollies. A little track fords it, with stepping-stones in attendance. *This is the turning point of the walk, a lovely spot to linger.* Across, the

13

invisible path forks. Commence the return by doubling back left, downstream. The way quickly narrows and the stream must be re-crossed, briefly. A few paces further, use a small gate to cross again on a small bridge, then head away from the stream, crossing the field to a corner stile. Here is another tiny bridge on a trickle, from which rise away with a hedge. Almost at once though, cross a stile to its other side and resume gently rising. This runs to a stile onto a back road.

Turn briefly right along the road, and at a bend take a gate on the left to follow a hedge away to the farm at Close House. Pass through a paddock at the end to join its drive, and cross straight over between house and barns to a gate into a yard. Here take another gate on the left and cross the centre of a large field. At the end drop left to a stile in the bottom. Another footbridge takes you across another drain, then resume away with a hedge on your right, soon levelling out and running through undergrowth on a long fieldside. Towards the end bear left to a large gap, and resume along the right side of a hedge. At the end it joins a grassy cart track between fine hedgerows.

The Durham Ox, Crayke

*Stained glass window,
St Cuthbert's church,
Crayke*

Go right just a few yards along it before resuming the Crayke bee-line on a broad hedgeside path. Crossing a bridge at the end bear gently left up the slope to a level track. Though the path strictly continues rising left, more common practice is to go briefly left along the track and then ascend the field-side on another broad path. Through the gap at the top corner take a bridle-gate on the left. Though the right-of-way slants left up towards the trees at the top before doubling back right, local usage sees a more direct rise up to a kissing-gate at the top. *Before entering the trees, pause to look back over a splendid prospect of the walk's landscape, the highlight being the Kilburn White Horse, with the dramatic scarp of Roulston Scar to its left.*

A well-used path heads off through trees to emerge in the churchyard. Pass round either side of the church before emerging either left (main access) or down a few steps at the end onto the road brow. *This gives a few steps' detour right to appraise both the castle and a spacious view over Easingwold and the Vale of York to a long Pennine skyline. The enormous and plentiful golf balls of the US Menwith Hill base beyond Harrogate can often be discerned with the naked eye.* Go left to finish.

3

CITY OF TROY

START *Scackleton*   *Grid ref. SE 647728*

DISTANCE *5¹⁄₂ miles (9km)*

ORDNANCE SURVEY MAPS
1:50,000
Landranger 100 - Malton & Pickering
1:25,000
Explorer 300 - Howardian Hills & Malton

ACCESS *Start from the village centre. Roadside parking. Served by infrequent Castle Howard-Malton bus.*

> *A magnificently varied walk featuring a maze, a beautiful old church, first-class valley surroundings and big views*

Scackleton is a remote farming village perched at a relatively elevated 377ft/115m on a brow of the Howardian Hills. A broad main street features attractive cottages, a pond at Manor Farm, a Victorian postbox and thatched cottages behind the old chapel, near where the old village pump occupies a roadside recess. Head east along the street with grass verge and footway to the church at the end. *The plain church of St George the Martyr dates from 1910, and has a new red pantile roof.* Here take the unsigned road branching right. *Open views look over the Plain of York to Sheriff Hutton Castle and beyond.* The road runs a pleasant fieldside course, dropping down to ultimately lose its surface. Just a few strides further it forks: with Low Moor Farm on your left, take the track straight on to Dalby Bush Farm. *Converted to residential use, its splendid range of buildings enjoy an idyllic seclusion.* After the house turn down to a footbridge and ford on Dalby Bush Beck.

Across, bear right to a gate in the fence ahead, and a stony track climbs the fieldside onto the narrow ridge-top road of High

Lane. Either go left a few strides then branch right down the side road, or a step-stile in front gives an open access option, bearing right over the brow and down the bank to a stile onto Low Lane, at Dalby. While the onward route is right, just to the left is St Peter's church. *This beautiful old building occupies an idyllic, peaceful setting, with its sloping churchyard looking out over the Vale of York. Though a substantial amount survives from its 12th century origins, most fascinating feature is the 600-year old chancel at the eastern end: appearing more like a fortified defensive structure, it has a barrel vaulted ceiling inside its 4-foot thick walls. The old rectory and the hall form the remainder of Dalby.*

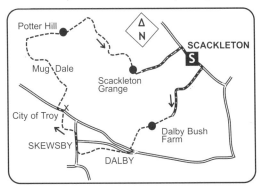

Back on the lane turn right just as far as the end of the house garden, then take a kissing-gate on the left. Turn right on a decent path along the top of a vast sloping, scrubby pasture. *Savour more comprehensive sweeping views over the plain.* Although strictly you contour across part way on, standard practice is to rise to the top corner then drop to a kissing-gate in the corner below. Descend past stone huts and an allotment to the gate below, then turn right along the field top, an improving hedgeside path running along all the way to the upper part of the hamlet of Skewsby. It is entered via a gate and along a short driveway onto the road.

Go right to the top end of the hamlet and at the junction continue up, climbing steeply through trees. The road is soon left when a broad grassy way heads into Brow Wood on the left. This swings left and fades, but a thin, clear path swings right. This runs

17

a delightful course through the wood, rising to finally emerge on the left near the top. Rise outside the final trees and cross to the unfenced road just ahead. Go left two minutes to discover the City of Troy. *This unsung gem is a rare and diminutive example of a turf maze, the origins of which go back many centuries, as does the intriguing name (illustrated on page 6). A seat looks over the maze and its scattering of spring daffodils to a quite stupendous view that includes the North York Moors, the Yorkshire Wolds and even a little of the Yorkshire Dales.*

Just a minute further turn right down a grassy track through open fields, reaching a junction above a wood corner. Go left on a splendid bridlepath descending through undergrowth into Mug Dale. Continue down increasingly deeply towards the dale bottom, swinging left to run a lovely course above the beck before meeting an access road in the trees. Turn right over the bridge then sharp left through a moist corner. A path climbs steeply up the bank of Mugdale Wood, easing out and running a splendid course along the plantation edge. Easing further it merges with a broad grassy way. Turn right on this through the gate and away along its grand hedgerowed course, slowly dropping down with big rolling views ahead to join the drive leading to Potter Hill Farm. *This attractive place boasts a fine arrangement of domestic and outbuildings.*

A barn at Scackleton Grange   Right: St Peter's church, Dalby

Pass between the buildings and bear right, down to a kissing-gate just below. Descend the field to another into the woods. A thin path drops down (initially steeply) through two small gates to a footbridge on the tiny beck. Bear right up the steep bank, but towards the top turn right past gorse bushes to a kissing-gate at the end. *The attractive surroundings hereabouts are notable for the profusion of broadleaved woodland.* Bear left towards the buildings at Swathgill, but without entering turn right down the distinct field centre trough. The stream is re-crossed on a wooden bridge, then bear left up the steep bank to emerge onto a distinctive crest. Drop left with the fence to a gate in the dip of the dry hollow, then head away bearing right to a clump of trees. These shelter Randale Spring, which gurgles gently from beneath the uppermost tree.

Bear right through this delectable gorse-flanked little valley. Crossing its sunken stream, a track forms to double back left up the bank to a gate at the top corner. With good views over the valley follow this track across a field to a gate at the end, where it swings right to run to Scackleton Grange. Head straight on through the colourful farmyard and past the house onto the track junction just beyond. Turn left and follow Grange Lane back out to the village, a pleasant stride with far-reaching views from its elevated course.

4

HOVINGHAM PARK

START Hovingham   Grid ref. SE 667755

DISTANCE 5^{1}4 miles (8^{1}2km)

ORDNANCE SURVEY MAPS
1:50,000
Landranger 100 - Malton & Pickering
1:25,000
Explorer 300 - Howardian Hills & Malton

ACCESS Start from the village centre on the B1257. Roadside parking and village hall car park. Served by Malton-Helmsley bus.

Attractive woodland and parkland fringing a classic village

Hovingham is a picture-postcard village with spacious greens sat between a rich variety of buildings and a lovely stream. The Worsley Arms Hotel is named from the family who built Hovingham Hall in 1563, and remain to this day in the present 18th century building. It opens to the public on afternoons for several weeks only from early June to early July, not Sundays. A second pub is the Malt Shovel, while there is also a shop and a popular tearoom/bakery. All Saints church was restored in the 1860s but retains an Anglo-Saxon tower, while there are attractive red-brick almshouses from 1870.

Leave the main street at its southern end, where the road swings sharp left to bend away past the almshouses. Instead take a short-cut path up a small green to join a road climbing away. This is quickly escaped by a hedgerowed cart track bearing left. With big views back to the North York Moors this splendid track rises gradually before leveling out to run on through open fields to approach South Wood. Within two minutes of entering keep straight on at a cross-track to a fork just beyond. Here bear left, gently declining and swinging right as it levels out. Here take a footpath dropping left, and a gate at the bottom puts you into the area known as Hollin Hill Bogs.

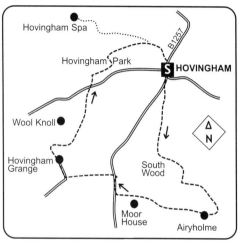

Cross the moist open area to a tiny bridge and stream, and from a bridle-gate behind bear left on a field-edge path outside the trees. At the far corner it delves into the wood, and runs a good course between Wath Beck and characterful bog. The improving path continues upstream with a field alongside, swinging right at the end to a bridleway junction by a grassy, stone-arched farm bridge. Don't cross but turn right on the grass track rising to Airyholme Farm. It keeps right of all buildings to join the drive. Turn right on this to run a pleasant, undulating course out to join the Hovingham-Sheriff Hutton road alongside Moor House Farm. *Your surroundings are archetypal rolling Howardian Hills country.*

Go right for a couple of minutes towards the woods, but take a gate on the left to descend a cart track to a stone bridge on a lively beck. A nicer green way ascends the fieldside beyond, running on to the bend of an access road. Turn right down this and up past Hovingham Lodge, a big mansion of Magnesian limestone. The firm track winds down the other side to a stone bridge on the beck.

Immediately across take a kissing-gate on the right, and a super path heads away downstream. The large house at Wool Knoll boasts a fine location up to the left. The path leads delightfully on through the valley to converging flanks, entering woodland with a pond on the other bank. Becoming a broad green way through the trees, ultimately this emerges onto the Hovingham-Coulton road.

The elegant bridge in Hovingham Park

Cross to a stile opposite and turn right to enjoy a lovely walk on a permissive route through Hovingham Park. Shortly the gurgling stream returns to lead you along to an elegant stone bridge across it. *Ahead is the imposing facade of Hovingham Hall. Looking back from the bridge, try to deny that the beck is not flowing uphill to here, an intriguing optical illusion!* The public footpath crosses the bridge from the roadside gate, so without crossing the bridge take the path rising left, joined by a track to pass through a gate on the brow. Now follow the right-hand fence the short way down to the corner, and from the stile turn right. A grand path heads through the ploughed field back towards Hovingham, over a footbridge on a dry drain, and along a hedgeside at the end to a driveway to farm buildings. From the stile ahead cross a paddock to a stile onto a road-end by a play area and burial ground on the edge of the village. *See below for an optional extension to Hovingham Spa.* Turn right to finish alongside the beck.

In Hovingham

A visit to Hovingham Spa entails an additional 2-mile return walk. Turn through the gate on the left and follow an enclosed grassy track away. Keep straight on at a cross-track, and the firm track runs on through flat, open fields. Ignoring a lesser left branch it eventually arrives at Spa Villa in the trees of Spa Plantation, the site of Hovingham Spa: the Victorians delighted in the restorative powers of mineral springs, though Hovingham never took off on any scale. The most distinct spring is 30 yards into the trees on the left after the house, a decent gurgle of water coming out from under a rock and forming a circular pool just yards further.

The ford, Hovingham

STONEGRAVE & THE RYE

START Nunnington   Grid ref. SE 669794

DISTANCE 6¼ miles (10km)

ORDNANCE SURVEY MAPS
1:50,000
Landranger 100 - Malton & Pickering
1:25,000
Explorer 300 - Howardian Hills & Malton

ACCESS Start from the village centre. Roadside parking (National Trust car park at the Hall). Served by Malton-Helmsley bus.

> The most varied walk on offer: a beautiful village, delectable riverbanks, an ancient church and an airy ridge with wide views

The village of Nunnington is a visual delight, sloping down to the River Rye with charming cottages sporting red pantile roofs and numerous hidden corners. In a beautiful riverside setting stands the National Trust property of Nunnington Hall. This lovely 17th century manor house is open to the public and sits amid delightful walled gardens, and also has a tearoom. Village pub is the Royal Oak, while there is a tearoom at Nunnington Studios, and adjacent gallery. At the top of the village is the 13th century church of St James & All Saints, restored in the 19th century but with a tower from 1672. The school of 1839 is now a private house.

From the crossroads by the bridge outside the Hall, turn up the York road for a few paces just as far as a drive on the left. Here a stile sends you up the field to a stile at the top, onto a driveway. Entering the grounds on the left (note the ha-ha), pass right of the house to a small gate in a beech hedge at the end. *A large gate on your left gives a fine view of the Hall.* From a second gate head along the field outside the wall beneath a distinct bank. Approaching an ornate gateway bear right to an ordinary gate, and on again. Though a grassy track slants up, bear left to a stile/gate ahead, with the Rye just to the left. Approach Mill Farm alongside the drained cut that once served it. *The former mill is a splendid old building looking over the farm buildings.*

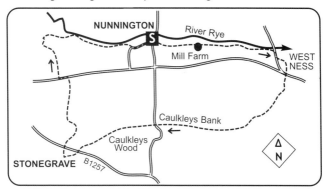

From a kissing-gate in front pass through the yard to another ahead, then along a fieldside to join the river. Now enjoy this level walk downstream on a lovely path. *The Rye begins life high on the North York Moors, and is second only to the Esk in the hierarchy of the National Park's rivers. Flowing 16 unspoilt miles to leave the National Park at Helmsley, it absorbs several other Moors' rivers on the flat Vale of Pickering before its own identity is lost in the Derwent just short of Malton. This is the only walk to savour its banks.* From a kissing-gate into a sheep pasture cut a bend of the river by bearing slightly right past ponds. Back with the Rye remain outside the wooded bank and resume, noting a crescent pond on the opposite bank. A pair of kissing-gates in quick succession lead onto the road at the concrete bridge at West Ness.

Turn right into the hamlet. *A forlorn building between the phone box and postbox is the former Wesleyan Methodist chapel of 1836.* Remain on the through road at a junction just beyond, and as you rise to a junction above, consider a stroll through the Woodland Trust's Joan's Wood on the left: from a small gate into it a path rises to emerge via a gate at the top. From the road bend immediately after the junction ascend an enclosed cart track. Beyond two barns it transforms into a classic hedgerowed green way. *This gem of a walk offers big views across to the Vale of Pickering, left, ahead to a Wolds skyline beyond the Earthworks Ridge, and also back to an extended North York Moors skyline.* Ultimately meeting an access track, cross straight over for a steady rise at the start of Caulkleys Bank.

This soon eases and begins another splendid march along the gentle domed ridge. *Caulkleys Bank is an intruder in the Howardians scene, for it is actually the parting shot of the Hambleton Hills, projecting from Oswaldkirk down to the Rye. It exerts itself sufficiently to breach the 100 metre mark, though the actual 'summit' is unmarked. Wide open views look to both sides: the relatively steep southern bank falls towards Hovingham and the Howardian Hills, while the gentle northern slopes look across to the North York Moors - note the huddled red roofs of the little*

towns of Helmsley and Kirkbymoorside. Towards the end a stone bench and a stone Ordnance Survey column at 321ft/98m are passed, and the track runs on to emerge at a popular parking area on the road summit on The Avenue.

Nunnington Hall

Cross straight over to resume on a good track. *An early branch right offers a short return.* The full route forges straight on, with Caulkleys Wood on your left and commencing a very gradual descent, ultimately losing the view. At the end bear left to a gate/stile in a gap in the trees, offering a big view over the vale beyond Stonegrave. A gem of a sunken way makes a steep descent of the bank, quickly giving a bird's-eye view over the village. Pass above a seat and along to a gate, just past which it joins the B1257 through the village. *Cottages to the right have an old quarry as their back gardens.*

Cross to the footway, drop left and then down the green to go right on a path accessing the church. *The lovely church of the Holy Trinity is better known as Stonegrave Minster, with origins as far back as the mid-8th century when it was one of several 'mother' churches, Coxwold included, from where St Aidan's followers spread Christianity. Its most celebrated feature is a beautifully carved Celtic cross discovered in 1862 within the church wall. The upper of two figures is supposedly that of Christ holding the Book of Life. Elsewhere within the church heraldry abounds, while an effigy thought to be of Sir John de Stonegrave is close by an early 15th century tomb of the influential Thornton family.*

Stonegrave Minster

Leave by a stile in the bottom corner of the churchyard, along to a bridle-gate into a field. Cross to the fence opposite (diverted path) then ascend to a kissing-gate at the top, rejoining the road. Cross straight over and take a gate to the left, from where a cart track ascends a steep pasture alongside a wooded dell. *Views look westwards to Oswaldkirk nestling beneath the Hambleton scarp, while the Howardians rise modestly across the Coxwold-Gilling gap behind you.* Easing at the top to run on to a corner, remain on the broad grass track swinging left along the field edge, and around to pass through a gap in the hedge. *Ahead now is a wide prospect of the Moors.* A steady hedgeside descent leads down onto a road. *For a shorter return, Nunnington is just ten minutes along to the right.*

Go briefly left then turn right down a firm hedgeside track. This zigzags past an unmapped plantation and along to a larger plantation corner. Here leave the track for a path branching right outside the trees. At the end go left through a gap in the trees into another field, then right along the hedgeside path to a sudden arrival at a big bend on the bank of the Rye. *This is a splendid moment worth lingering over.* All that remains is to shadow the river downstream, starting by crossing a bridge on a side drain. The path traces the bank through several fields, the penultimate one from a bridle-gate being more direct than the river. At the end of the final field a kissing-gate puts you back into the village alongside a river bridge. The street directly ahead will lead you along the village-foot back to the Hall.

The River Rye approaching Nunnington

SLINGSBY BANKS

START *Slingsby   Grid ref. SE 698748*

DISTANCE *5³4 miles (9km)*

ORDNANCE SURVEY MAPS
1:50,000
Landranger 100 - Malton & Pickering
1:25,000
Explorer 300 - Howardian Hills & Malton

ACCESS *Start from the village centre off the B1257. Roadside parking. Served by Malton-Helmsley bus.*

Leisurely walking on and around the Earthworks Ridge: big views

    Slingsby is a popular village that is a favourite of the caravan fraternity. A maypole adorns the central green between the village school and a Wesleyan Methodist Chapel of 1837. Also on offer are the Grapes pub, a restaurant, a village shop and a bakery at the old station. The broad main street has some fine dwellings set back from grass verges. All Saints church was restored in the 19th century and includes a 14th century memorial to a knight. A more secretive building is Slingsby Castle: this 14th century fortified manor house later became a Jacobean mansion, and though engulfed in trees its remains are visible from the roadside.

From the green take the Malton road east and then south (The Balk) up to the B1257. Go straight across, but as it bends left head straight up an inviting hedgerowed cart track. This is Bank Lane, which rises pleasantly to emerge into a field. Go left, briefly, then the path swings right across the field centre to a bridle-gate into Slingsby Banks Wood. Joining a good path go right on its splendid wood-edge course with views out to the North York Moors.

A bridleway crossroads is reached just after a plantation begins on the right. Turn left on a path down the wooded bank. *To the left is evidence of the bank and ditch of the Intrenchment earthwork, an ancient ridgetop defensive feature better revealed in WALK 7.* Initially amid bracken, the path broadens to drop down through a clearing. *In springtime primroses, bluebells and wild garlic are displayed here.* A little lower the path emerge out of the trees onto a bridleway crossroads at Hall Moor. *Just in front are the distinct grassy mounds of two tumuli, ancient burial mounds.*

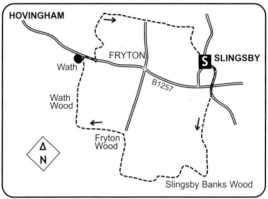

Turn right on an excellent grass track between new plantings and the wood bottom. Beyond the plantings it swings left to a gate and through the centre of a vast pasture all the way to join a firm track. Turn right, re-entering the wood and climbing to a crossroads back on the ridge. *The Moors return ahead, with the red-roofed huddle of Kirkbymoorside prominent.* Fryton Lane offers a short-cut down to the B1257, but your way rejoins the ridge-top path by turning left above Fryton West Wood, initially with trees all around. After the right side opens out it drops to a corner and fork at Hollin Hill, with a bridle-gate on the right. Turn through this to leave the trees, and a fieldside path runs on outside Wath Wood. The wood turns away, a quarry appears ahead, and the improving path runs on to its near corner. This superb green way descends outside the quarry. *Though largely screened, a short spell reveals the extent of this operation to win limestone. Hovingham village*

is seen to the left. Through a gate at the bottom another track is joined to drop past a recolonised quarry to a gate onto the B1257 at Wath. *Business units opposite include the base of the AONB.*

Turn right up the broad verge, quickly crossing to a bridle-gate opposite. Descend to one just below, then on a few strides to a track alongside rusting farm machinery. Take the track bearing right to a farm bridge, then go left to the field corner. Now dead-flat, the fieldside path turns sharp right to the far corner Here is a crossroads with a footpath on the course of the old Thirsk & Malton branch of the North Eastern Railway.

Turn right on the more inviting path, and this leads back to Slingsby, seen ahead. As a broader track takes over, its embanked course is more obvious and makes a grand stride. An access road is crossed at a cottage, and the old track resumes beyond a Fryton mosaic. Shortly after passing a tree-shrouded pond on the left (and with the road in sight ahead) a nicer finish presents itself. From a bridle-gate on the right a path runs alongside a garden to the drive ahead. Remain on this, absorbing others, to run out over Lawns Bridge and along past Slingsby Hall and sports fields to re-enter the village alongside the church. Go right a few yards on High Street, noting the castle, then left along The Green to finish.

Slingsby Castle

7

CONEYSTHORPE BANKS

START *Barton-le-Street*   *Grid ref. SE 721742*

DISTANCE *6¹⁄4 miles (10km)*

ORDNANCE SURVEY MAPS
1:50,000
Landranger 100 - Malton & Pickering
1:25,000
Explorer 300 - Howardian Hills & Malton

ACCESS *Start from the village centre just off the B1257. Roadside parking by the greens. Served by Malton-Helmsley bus.*

> *A splendid march along the historic and well wooded
> Earthworks Ridge, with sweeping views*

Barton-le-Street is one of several villages with such an appendage, the 'Street' in question being the B1257 Malton road, which runs beneath the northern scarp of the Howardian Hills and links a whole string of villages, all of which spread along the flatter ground north of the Street. The church of St Michael & All Angels dates from 1871, a simple structure of local limestone and featuring a double bell-cote. From the former smithy on the main road descend past the church and down to the centre.

Past the village hall more spacious greens open out. Continue past the main green and swing round to the right, on past a further green and along to a junction at the village edge. Turn right on the private-looking road signed Glebe Farm, passing the farm and along to a sharp bend right. Here go straight ahead along a hedgerowed rough road, continuing straight on when the main way turns left. The grass continuation fades along the fieldside but advance to successive small gates at the end. Now slant up the paddock to a gate at the top corner, from where an enclosed track rises away and runs on past a former limestone quarry to emerge onto the Street on the edge of Appleton-le-Street. The broad verge is quickly replaced by a welcome footpath. Watch out for steps on the right guiding you up into a corner of the churchyard. *The church of All Saints boasts a superb Anglo-Saxon tower, while inside are two 700-year old female effigies.* Past the church a back lane is joined to drop left to a junction of such lanes just yards from the main road. *Here stands the village pub, the Cresswell Arms.*

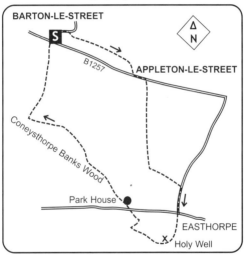

Your route continues by turning right up the side lane from the pub. At an immediate fork go straight ahead up a hedgerowed lane, rising gently out of the village into a field. Remain on this until it ends at a gap in a field boundary. Now level, the way properly slants left to the far corner, though common practice is to go left on the accommodating verge and then alongside some gallops to the corner. *Massive views look left across the Vale of Pickering to the North York Moors.* Here a firm hedgeside track is joined, running left along another fieldside to the brow of a narrow road, Amotherby Lane. Turn right on the accommodating verge to the junction alongside a lodge at Easthorpe.

Cross to a drive just yards to the right (not the thin path straight ahead), and head directly away ignoring a branch for Easthorpe Stud. The firm track enjoys a delightful descent into woodland. Just before emerging you pass the Holy Well in a hollow on the right. *Here water emerges into a stone trough only to return immediately to its subterranean course.* Through the gate ahead turn sharp right on the enclosed bridleway outside the trees, dropping down to the rear of a settlement with characterful red pantile roofs. This diversion from older maps runs along the rear of the buildings and resumes on a very pleasant fieldside course by Spring Wood. *Over to the left is the domed top of Castle Howard.*

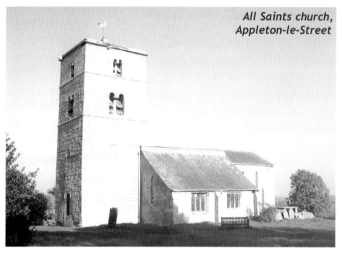

All Saints church, Appleton-le-Street

Remain on this wood-edge course until a sharp corner, where turn right on a thin path to a gate in the corner. Here an inviting grassy way rises steeply up the newly planted bank on Hepton Hill, a steep haul by Howardians standards, winding up to seats and then along to a gate onto the Coneysthorpe-Malton road. Cross straight over onto the Park House drive, but take a bridle-gate on the left before the restored courtyard converted to business use. *Archetypal Howardian Hills parkland drops away to the left.* A thin path skirts round the outside of the grounds to cross to the corner behind. Pass through a gap in the trees to go clearly left, another wood-edge course on the crest of Coneysthorpe Banks. In contrast to the gentle slopes on your right, the wooded bank of the Intrenchments Ridge drops steeply left. *This ancient earthwork of bank and ditch was built for defensive purposes, and stretches for several miles along the main Howardian Hills ridge.*

The path runs a super course for some time, later entering a colourful copse and emerging with more open views as the field drops more markedly away. At the end the path enters woodland, briefly, to reach a crossroads of ways. Forge straight on along the inviting grassy ride on the crest. The particularly distinctive ditch and bank of the earthwork is now a constant companion. Well before reaching the plantation ahead a junction is reached. Turn right through a bridle-gate and head away on a super fieldside path again that slowly declines from the ridge. *Ahead are panoramic views across Rye Dale to the moors; towards the bottom Barton village clusters around its church. Your route underfoot is Kirk Road, by which the residents of Coneysthorpe accessed the church at Barton.* Reaching the bottom the path swings right, and part way along drops down onto a short driveway back onto the B1257 in Barton.

Barton-le-Street

CASTLE HOWARD

START *Welburn   Grid ref. SE 721680*

DISTANCE *5¹⁄₂ miles (9km)*

ORDNANCE SURVEY MAPS
1:50,000
Landranger 100 - Malton & Pickering
1:25,000
Explorer 300 - Howardian Hills & Malton

ACCESS *Start from the village centre. Roadside parking. Served by York-Malton bus.*

> *An absorbing walk discovering myriad features spread around the parkland of one of the great stately homes: consider a morning walk followed by a full visit*

Welburn is a pleasant street village of many nice old cottages, featuring the Crown & Cushion pub and a tearoom. The spired church of St John dates from 1858. The old reading room retains a working clock complete with a chiming bell in its roof canopy next to the well-named Sundial House. Head west along the street, and after the very last house on the right take a rough access road dropping away. Go straight down this past a group of big storage barns on the right, soon improving into a grassy cart track. *The Pyramid on the Castle Howard estate is visible on the skyline.*

Lower down the track turns right through the hedge to cross a field. Quickly leave by taking a path left at a guidepost, dropping to a hedge corner and then pleasantly down the fieldside to a gap in the scrub at the bottom. Across the bridge and up the other side a grassy path heads away to a corner gate. Ahead is a ruinous tower by the estate wall. Advance on the hedgeside as far as a kissing-gate and go left with the hedge to Moor Houses Farm.

From a kissing-gate into the yard cross to one ahead, then on the enclosure to a corner one. Now drop right to one at the bottom of the field, from where a path ascends the rough bank to the ruined tower. *These semi-circular remains are the first of several 1720s mock fortifications that straddle the old estate wall. Just along to the right is the Pyramid: this was built in 1728 by Nicholas Hawksmoor, and contains a large bust of Lord William Howard. Look back for a good view past Welburn to the Wolds.* Just beyond the tower you join a surfaced estate road.

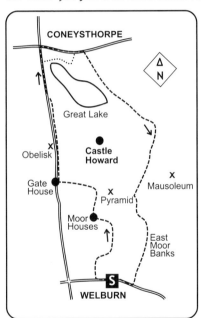

Castle Howard can be viewed by turning a minute to the right, but it will be seen later in the walk. Further right is the Mausoleum, with which you will also later see closer. Castle Howard is one of the great Yorkshire estates. The resplendent house was built between 1701 and 1731 for Charles Howard, the third Earl of Carlisle by the acclaimed architect John Vanbrugh. Still remembered as the setting for the TV drama 'Brideshead Revisited', it is open to the public and also has some beautiful gardens and grounds to leisurely explore, along with a number of shops and cafes.

Turn left along the road, making use of a grass verge to meet The Avenue alongside the impressive Gate House. *Designed by Vanbrugh in 1719 with the wings added later, this long building features a central archway crowned by a stone pyramid, and bears the Howard arms and a Latin inscription. At one time an inn, note the redundant Victorian postbox occupying the recess. Look* through this (with care!) to see the 120ft/36m Carlisle Memorial Column almost a mile and a half to the south. *Designed by Frederick Cockerell, it was erected in 1869 in memory of George, the 7th Earl of Carlisle.* Turn right along The Avenue with a choice of very broad grass verge or parallel path in the trees, certainly there is no need to tread tarmac. *Lined with stately trees The Avenue was laid out to form a fitting approach to the newly built Castle Howard. The road dips and rises to the Obelisk, which fills the centre of the road at the entrance to Castle Howard. This was erected in 1714 to commemorate the Duke of Marlborough's war victories.*

The Gate House on The Avenue

Continue straight on, dipping down to cross the Obelisk Ponds. With the Great Lake appearing to the right the road rises away, and a narrower, open verge leads to the very corner of the lake, where a kissing-gate offers a permissive path option along the shore. Just after swinging right there is a branch down into Lakeside Holiday Park. By turning right a few yards and then left past the toilet block, another left turn takes you out onto the road on the edge of Coneysthorpe. Should that option not be taken then continue to the crossroads ahead with ornate gateposts and a lodge of 1874, and turn right for the short stroll into Coneysthorpe, with a verge then a footway. *This attractive estate village spreads along to the left, either side of a broad green. At the far end is a restored chapel, with a charming plain interior open to view. Sporting a canopied bell-cote it was built in 1835 as a chapel of ease in the parish of Barton-le-Street, to which it was linked by an old track known as the Kirk Road. The village hall of 1852 was originally the school.*

Coneysthorpe Chapel

Just after the last house take a tall gate on the right, this accesses a firm track which runs on through the estate grounds. The big house is seen ahead, on a rise. Remain on this to the start of trees on the right, where a faint grassy path slants left to cut a corner of the track. Rejoining it at a guidepost, cross straight over and off along a much clearer path through scrub and scattered birches on the edge of Ray Wood. This runs a parallel course outside the old inner estate boundary wall, keep on until joining a firm track. Go right on this through a gate and out from the trees into open parkland. At a corner just ahead the more obvious way is up the wallside track to the Temple on the brow, but the right of way runs faintly into the centre to a guidepost by a reedy pond. Here rise right through an old ridge and furrow field system to the brow.

The elegant Temple Of The Four Winds was designed by Vanbrugh, and features a dome and four porticos. Completed in 1738, it was restored in 1955 as one of George Howard's post-War projects. Although it stands inside the grounds of the house it is well seen from your route. Below is the New River Bridge, with the Mausoleum on the hill beyond. *This hugely impressive circular building was designed by Hawksmoor and built between 1729 and 1741. It features a chapel and a crypt containing 63 niches for receiving coffins, and remains the family burial site.*

Descend the faint track to the bridge. *This mighty structure crosses the pond of New River and seems a little extravagant for the likes of us! It also gives the best view of the Mausoleum and a neat prospect of the house, with the Temple and the Pyramid also on display.* The track rises to meet the estate road from earlier in the walk. Turn left a few strides and turn up the track to a gate into the woods at East Moor Banks. *Look back for a last view of the great house.*

Take the broad path slanting down through the trees between dense carpets of springtime bluebells to a bridge on Moorhouse Beck, and briefly up the other side to a bridle-gate out into a field. With Welburn just ahead a good track runs on to a track crossroads, going straight ahead on the fieldside cart track to drop to the end of Water Lane. Rise up this to re-enter the village street alongside Sundial House.

Castle Howard

AROUND TERRINGTON

START *Terrington Grid ref. SE 670706*

DISTANCE *6 miles (9$\frac{1}{2}$km)*

ORDNANCE SURVEY MAPS
1:50,000
Landranger 100 - Malton & Pickering
1:25,000
Explorer 300 - Howardian Hills & Malton

ACCESS *Start from the village centre. Roadside parking. Served by infrequent Castle Howard-Malton bus.*

Leisurely walking in the colourful hinterland of a lovely village

Terrington is a hugely attractive village, its main street and parallel back streets lined by neat cottages, with the old village pump situated on the top green. It has a pub, the Bay Horse, and a shop with gallery and tearoom. The lovely church of All Saints dates in part from the 12th century, with a 15th century tower. Alongside is Terrington Hall, which was built as a rectory in 1827 and is currently a preparatory school. Just outside the village is Yorkshire Lavender, a lavender farm and herb nursery with gift shop, tearoom and various attractions.

Leave the village by its eastern end, out on the tree-shaded road as far as a junction sporting an old signpost. Ignoring both branches take the enclosed green way of Broates Lane in between. Towards the end it narrows and through a small copse emerges into a field. *An extensive wooded landscape dominates to the left.* Advance straight on to the far end and a gateway beneath a wood corner. Continue outside the trees (note the old pond inside) to a kissing-gate into a better pasture. Advance to the next one at the wood corner just ahead, meeting a bridleway. Don't pass through but go left on the short-lived track to the fence corner. Now bear left over this sheep pasture to a fieldside drain leading to the fence corner ahead, turning right with the fence to the base of Cum Hag Wood. *This extensive broadleaved wood has revealed shy Roe deer on my visits.* Through a bridle-gate go left to follow the wood edge all the way round to eventually rise onto a bridle-gate onto a road.

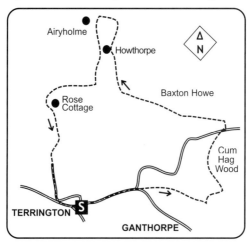

Turn right for just fifty paces and take a path climbing through trees on the left to join a forest road. Turn left on this for the best part of a mile along a broad ridge through non-claustrophic mixed woodland. *Gaps on the right permit views out, these becoming permanent as the wood ends. This fine prospect looks north over Baxton Howe and further plantations to a North York Moors skyline, while the White Horse of Kilburn is revealed ahead. The departure of trees from the left reveals a more intimate Howardian Hills landscape, as a flowery bank drops more steeply and Terrington is seen on the skyline.* The track which merges with another at the end to swing right to Howthorpe Farm.

Turn right down the near side of the extensive farmyard, and an initially enclosed track departs to descend a field towards woodland at the bottom. Here turn left on the fieldside path outside the trees to a corner gate into a sheep pasture. Just ahead is another gate on a path junction by a grassy, stone-arched farm bridge on Wath Beck. Don't pass through but double back left up the steep pasture. *Two pronounced banks and a ditch are part of an ancient site.* Rise left to the bank, and when level with the farmhouse again take a gate in the fence. *Terrington's church tower sits on the skyline ahead.* Turn right away from the farm, descending with the fence to a gate at the bottom. Cross a parallel track and slant across the field to a gate/stile by the tree-lined Wath Beck.

Advance along the part moist pasture as far as a footbridge, crossing this but not the adjoining half over a small drain. Instead take the bridle-gate in between and ascend the slope on a broad fieldside path. Towards the top look back for a fine prospect over Howthorpe, then the track swings left and onto the top. Continue

through a gate on the fading track, and bear right with the fence to join another track just above Rose Cottage Farm. Leave the track at once for a gate opposite, from which a grassy path avoids the house by running parallel to the right. Down the slope the path rejoins the drive, noting the big pond of Low Water ahead. Crossing Sawmill Beck the drive rises away, becoming surfaced as it climbs to the edge of the village.

All Saints church, Terrington

MOWTHORPE

START *Bulmer   Grid ref. SE 697675*

DISTANCE *5^{1}4 miles (8^{1}2km)*

ORDNANCE SURVEY MAPS
1:50,000
Landranger 100 - Malton & Pickering
1:25,000
Explorer 300 - Howardian Hills & Malton

ACCESS *Start from the village centre. Roadside parking. Served by York-Malton and Castle Howard-Malton bus.*

A fine mix of colourful woods break up the Mowthorpe landscape

 Bulmer is a lovely street village with attractive cottages set back from open greens. St Martin's church dates in part from the 11th century with a 15th century tower, and its surprisingly plain interior contains an effigy of Sir John Bulmer dating from about 1270. Leave the village at its western end, where a cart track turns right before the last house, Kilburn House. This descends to a pair of gates, below which a hedgeside path drops to a footbridge on a tree-lined beck. Across, bear left up the pasture to a corner gate, from where a broad path rises with a hedge on your left. Over a gentle brow with open views, from the end a thin path crosses a field centre to a bridle-gate into Ox Pasture Wood. *This pleasant woodland is carpeted with springtime bluebells.* A path slants down to a footbridge at the bottom, and a grassy path heads away alongside two lakes at Birkdale Fishery. Opening out into a field advance straight on to a path junction in front of a hedge. Turn right on the track, but approaching Low Mowthorpe double back right down a short-lived driveway to a bridge by a smaller lake.

Don't cross the bridge but take a stile on the left and head upstream into Mowthorpe Dale, beneath a steep grass bank outside the wood. A stile at the end sends a path into the trees, quickly leaving by a stile after a footbridge on the stream. Entering a field corner remain on the path rising inside the trees and along beyond the brow. Towards the far corner take a bridle-gate in the adjacent fence and bear right up the pasture. Before the corner gate bear right through a gap in the scrub and cross the bank to rejoin the stream, passing beneath the house at Mowthorpe Dale. A grand ramble now ensues through this well-defined little valley, simply following the scrub-lined stream to the dalehead. Through a bridle-gate the stream gives up the ghost, and a grassy way crosses to a bridle-gate onto a hedgerowed track, Sleigh Lane. *The charming hamlet of Ganthorpe is just minutes along to the right.*

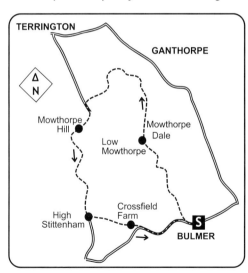

Turn left just as far as a sharp bend left: here turn right on a hedgeside path running to the corner then left to the next corner. From the junction of paths here go left, briefly along the third side of the field to a gate onto a grassy stone bridge on the adjacent tiny stream. Just a few steps to the left resume up the near side of the stream. When a hedge takes over pass to the other side to resume on an improving headland path to meet narrow Mowthorpe Lane. Go left the short way to a fork and bear right on the drive to Mowthorpe Hill Farm.

At this austere grouping go straight ahead to a hand-gate, along a paddock side and by the grassy hummocks of old quarries to the top corner of Mowthorpe Wood. *From the gate to your right note the extensive view across a colourful bank to the plains.* From a gate into the wood a broad path slants left down to a kissing-gate. In springtime the wooded bank below the path is massed with wild garlic. Emerging, you have an open prospect of Stittenham Wood, your next objective across the flat plain. A broad embanked green way slants down beneath the rest of the wood to meet a good track. *This section of wood is alive with springtime bluebells, while Bulmer's church tower is prominent on the skyline straight ahead.* Turn right through the gate and follow the track's hedgeside course down to its demise after bridging the deep drain of Ings Beck. Advance straight on to the clump of trees ahead, to the right of which is a wooden farm bridge on a more substantial drain. *To my delight a barn owl took off from beneath this bridge and watched me from a branch for some time. The tall remains of Sheriff Hutton Castle are silhouetted over to the right.*

Ox Pasture Wood from Bulmer   Opposite: Stittenham Pond

Cross the field to a track ascending through Stittenham Wood. This quickly swings sharp left, but your way is the thin path climbing ahead. *More bluebells are on show here.* Crossing a fainter old grass track, move a few steps right then resume uphill. Meeting a broader track drop briefly right on it, then turn sharp left on the re-ascending footpath. At the top High Stittenham appears and just short of the end the path diverts briefly left to leave the wood at a small gate. An enclosed garden side path emerges via the drive onto Stittenham's access road. *The hamlet of High Stittenham is a Piccadilly Circus of paths and tracks.*

Cross to the gate in front and use a stile alongside the pond. Slant up to another just above then a faint track heads left over the brow, making for a small gate in the hedge corner ahead. *Bulmer re-appears on the skyline ahead, while to the right are the Wolds.* Now bear right down the hedgeside, at the end bearing briefly left with the fence before taking a bridle-gate in it. Bear left again down this inviting pasture to approach Crossfield Farm. A small gate puts you onto a track just above the buildings. In front of the house use gates ahead to cross the farmyard. Emerging, take a small gate on the right and slant down the paddock to one below, just behind which another puts you onto the road on Stittenham Hill. Descend to cross Bulmer Beck by Bulmer Bridge and conclude with a short, steep ascent back into Bulmer.

SHERIFF HUTTON

START *Sheriff Hutton*   *Grid ref. SE 651663*

DISTANCE *6¹2 miles (10¹2km)*

ORDNANCE SURVEY MAPS
1:50,000
Landranger 100 - Malton & Pickering
1:25,000
Explorer 300 - Howardian Hills & Malton

ACCESS *Start from the village centre. Roadside parking and village hall car park. Served by York-Malton bus.*

A pleasant stroll from a colourful, historic village on the only walk entirely outside the AONB

Sheriff Hutton is a very pleasant village dominated, like the surrounding plain, by its castle ruins. Built as a fortified manor house in the late 14th century, it was already ruinous by the early 17th century. A tall tower stood at each corner and a gatehouse was added shortly after. Substantial sections of the two western towers survive, along with the gatehouse and fragmentary remains of the eastern towers and walls that enclosed a central courtyard. On private land but perfectly seen from the path, they might be inspected in closer detail by prior arrangement on 01347-878341.

Along the main street an extensive village green features stocks, and this once important settlement was granted a market charter in 1378. There are two pubs, the Castle Inn and the Highwayman, and a Post office/shop. The splendid church of St Helen & the Holy Cross stands at the very eastern end. Dating back in part to the 12th century and restored by the Nevilles in the 15th century, its prized feature is the supposed 15th century tomb of

Richard III's son, Edward, Prince of Wales. It also boasts medieval glass. From the central crossroads head east along Main Street past the shop. On the brow turn right on the Castle Farm drive, but before entering take a kissing-gate on the right with the castle ruins now looming above you. You can see all you need from the path, which runs on past the former moat. At the far end a kissing-gate sends a short snicket between houses out onto Finkle Street.

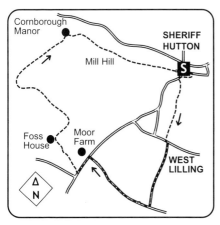

Turn briefly left on the footway, and at the bend by the village hall take a stile set back on the left. Ignore the firm track and follow the grassy hedgeside way on your right. *The castle is particularly well seen from here.* Use a stile part way along to resume on the other side by sports fields. At the end advance straight on a near bee-line through several fields, meeting a wooden footbridge and then a surfaced driveway as the houses of West Lilling appear just ahead. A hidden corner stile leads into the last field to cross to a short-lived green way down onto the road in West Lilling. *This unassuming hamlet features archetypal local architecture, with red-brick cottages sporting red pantile roofs.*

Go left a few strides then right along a narrow back road. After a kink you encounter an actual gradient, dropping down with views to the Plain of York and across to the Wolds escarpment. The road runs through open fields to a crossroads. *The road is as traffic-free as it gets, my encounters being with a pedestrian, an equestrian and a cyclist.* Turn right all the way along to a T-junction. Go left past Moor Farm to Sheriff Hutton Bridge, with its adjacent cricket ground. *The stream is the tiny River Foss, meandering southwards towards its entry into the Ouse in the heart of York.* Immediately over the bridge delve right down steps into undergrowth, and a thin path traces the sluggish beck upstream. Beyond the cricket ground a broader grassy way continues pleasantly along to an access road. Turn right over the stream and past Foss House with its delightful courtyard arrangement. Advance along the rough road as far as a junction, where turn left. With gentle slopes above, this similar track leads all the way to Cornborough Farm.

St Helen & the Holy Cross, Sheriff Hutton

Immediately after the buildings turn right to find a bridle-gate set back, and cross to another in the corner behind (ignoring a stile just to its left). Turn left with the drain to a gateway into a field, then sharp right up the hedgeside. An improving track remains underfoot, gradually rising to enter a sloping sheep pasture. This rises past a pond (more gradients!) to join the drive outside the equestrian setting of Cornborough Manor. *Note the ditch on the left outside the farm: this rectangular moat surrounded Bergh Castle, a 13th century fortified manor house of the de Thwengs.*

Turn right along the access road as far as the entrance to an electricity sub-station. From a corner kissing-gate pass along its perimeter and into a field. Cross this and another to a plank bridge then on past Mill Hill Farm to a kissing-gate further right at the far end. Ahead, the castle beckons. Follow fieldsides out into an open field, crossing to a pair of stiles at the corner. Resume alongside a distinctive ridge and furrowed field, maintaining this line until a clearer path enters a charming, leafy enclosed green way. This soon emerges onto Mill Lane at the edge of the village. Keep straight on past the school back into the centre.

Sheriff Hutton Castle   *Above: Highwayman, Sheriff Hutton*

RIVER DERWENT

START Kirkham   Grid ref. SE 734658

DISTANCE 5^{1}4 miles (8^{1}2km)

ORDNANCE SURVEY MAPS
1:50,000
Landranger 100 - Malton & Pickering
1:25,000
Explorer 300 - Howardian Hills & Malton

ACCESS Start from the priory ruins. Roadside and layby parking.

> A richly varied walk featuring a romantic monastic ruin,
> a hidden village and a superb unbroken riverside ramble

The hamlet of Kirkham occupies an enviable setting in a deep curve of the River Derwent downstream from Malton. Principal feature is the delectably sited ruin of Kirkham Priory on the riverbank. Founded in 1130 by Walter l'Espec for Augustinian monks, it survived until 1539, when at the Dissolution Prior John Kildwick had 17 canons in residence. It is in the care of English Heritage and open to the public. Outside the gatehouse is an ancient three-tiered cross. Manor Farm stands opposite, while the Stone Trough Inn is two minutes up the hill. The ancient Kirkham Bridge spans the river with three mellow stone arches: an old stone bearing an intriguing inscription has been incorporated in the south-eastern parapet at the start of the bridge. Kirkham once had its own rail station on this surviving branch of the North Eastern Railway's York-Scarborough line.

Start by crossing the bridge and then the level crossing, and as the road climbs away take a hand-gate on the left. A path ascends through Oak Cliff Wood, initially muddy after rain but the steeper upper section is far better. *In season these upper banks are graced with a superb bluebell carpet.* Emerging into a field at the top, bear right onto a back road. *Seen further right is the church spire of Whitwell-on-the-Hill.* With broad verges turn left, enjoying immediate views over Crambe sequestered in its hollow. Soon after the church tower appears, take a gate on the right from where a grassy way crosses the field past a small pond. From a kissing-gate at the end bear left past a house to join the little street.

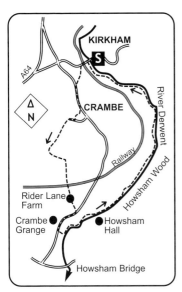

Crambe is as sleepy as they come. Along to the left is the church of St Michael dating in part from the 11th century, with a 15th century tower. A tiny one-roomed building just before it was the former school, its inscription telling of its erection by one Colonel Cholmley in 1813. Your route is right, along the street just as far as a kink. Pass through a gate by a cottage on the left, and out through another into a field at the rear. Head away with the hedge to drop down to a bridle-gate and footbridge on a stream. Rise away through another such gate in a few trees, and ascend the hedge-side to join a cart track. *This is an old byway linking Crambe and Barton-le-Willows on the plain below.* Advance along this onto a brow. *Big views look ahead to the dead-flat plain, with the Howardian Hills around to the right.*

Just after a track joins from the right, leave the byway as it commences an inviting descent. From a gate on the left head away with the hedgerow along the crest of Crambe Bank, a delightful stride atop a grassy sheep pasture. *Far-reaching views look ahead to the Wolds skyline, with the red-roofed huddle of Barton-le-Willows on the wide plain below.* Pass through a gate and resume

53

with a band of woodland on your left. When the trees end turn sharp right to descend the field centre to a bridle-gate in the hedge below. *Crambe Bank exhibits a classic ridge and furrow system: this is the result of a system of ploughing that has been used for many centuries, examples hereabouts possibly dating from medieval times.* From the gate a good hedgeside path runs along to meet the railway. Cross with care and along to Rider Lane Farm (formerly Railway House). Pass right of the house and its short drive leads out onto a back road, Riders Lane.

Kirkham Priory

Turn right through open fields, soon enjoying a section with neat hedges and verges beneath Crambe Grange. Returning to open fields turn left along a hedgeside to reach the bank of the River Derwent. *The Derwent is the principal river of East Yorkshire, beginning life high on Fylingdales Moor in the North York Moors National Park and joining the Ouse at Barmby-on-the-Marsh, near Goole.* Turning left, upstream, route directions effectively end: simply remain tight by the river all the way back to the start.

This classic ramble never leaves the riverbank and meets only the odd moist moment as you shadow the serene meanderings of the Derwent. *An early feature is Howsham Hall on the opposite bank, a large Jacobean mansion that served as a school for half a century until 2007. This is followed by the extensive Howsham Wood. Some sections of this walk look particularly remote, with plentiful woodland and only the odd building in sight. The sound of a passing train may surprise you as the railway winds cleverly around the bank just above.* Towards the end a scrubby area announces convergence with the railway, and a bridge on a final sidestream reveals the priory ahead. At a wide weir you emerge into a riverside pasture leading to a kissing-gate at the bridge.

Kirkham Bridge

INDEX *(walk number refers)*

WALK LOG

WALK	DATE	NOTES
1		
2		
3		
4		
5		
6		
7		
8		
9		
10		
11		
12		